A DAY ABOVE
OMAN

By John Nowell

Published with the support and encouragement of BP Middle East.

Motivate Publishing

Dedicated to
His Majesty Sultan Qaboos bin Said Al-Said
and the people of Oman

Published by Motivate Publishing

PO Box 2331, Dubai, UAE
Tel: 824060, Fax: 824436

PO Box 43072, Abu Dhabi, UAE
Tel: 311666, Fax: 311888

London House
26/40, Kensington High Street
London W8 4PF
Tel: (071) 938 2222, Fax: (071) 937 7293

Directors:
Obaid Humaid Al Tayer
Ian Fairservice

First printed 1990
Second impression 1991
First revised edition 1992
Reprinted 1993

ISBN 1 873544 30 8

Printed by Emirates Printing Press, UAE

His Majesty Sultan Qaboos bin Said Al-Said

Foreword

The Sultanate of Oman has inspired visitors for centuries with its beauty and diversity. Within the borders of one country can be found green hills and valleys, sandy beaches, coral reefs in an emerald-blue sea, rugged mountains and vast, moving desert. Once seen, never forgotten is an expression perfectly suited to Oman.

Until the accession of His Majesty Sultan Qaboos in 1970, this wonderful natural environment mostly lay dormant, but in the years since 1970, it has been harnessed for the good of the growing nation.

A mark of the wisdom of Oman's leaders is the way in which development has been woven into the fabric of the country: In John Nowell's superb aerial photography we have a record of how Oman's modern infrastructure and amenities have become a part of the landscape, and integral aspects of the lives of Omanis.

For more than 30 years, BP has played its part in Oman's progress. We are proud of our association with the Sultanate over the decades and of our commitment to protecting and enhancing its natural and human environment.

A Day Above Oman is a fitting tribute to these years of progress; in documenting the past and present it provides a clear blueprint to a bright future. We at BP hold great hope for this future and look forward to playing our part in it.

P M Willis

Contents

Front cover: A Royal Flight helicopter gives its passengers a bird's eye view of the huge collapsed limestone cavern at Tawi Attair, meaning the Cave of Birds. By chance, sunlit reflections from the pool were caught at the instant of exposure. Endpapers: The straight-winged shadows of flamingoes are sharply outlined on mud flats near Masirah. Title page: The Hokuf Ridge marks the eastern boundary of the Jiddat Al Harrisis. Back cover: Stark beauty in the sweep of a sand dune in the Rub Al Khali. This page: A Puma helicopter of The Royal Flight sets out in the first light of dawn.

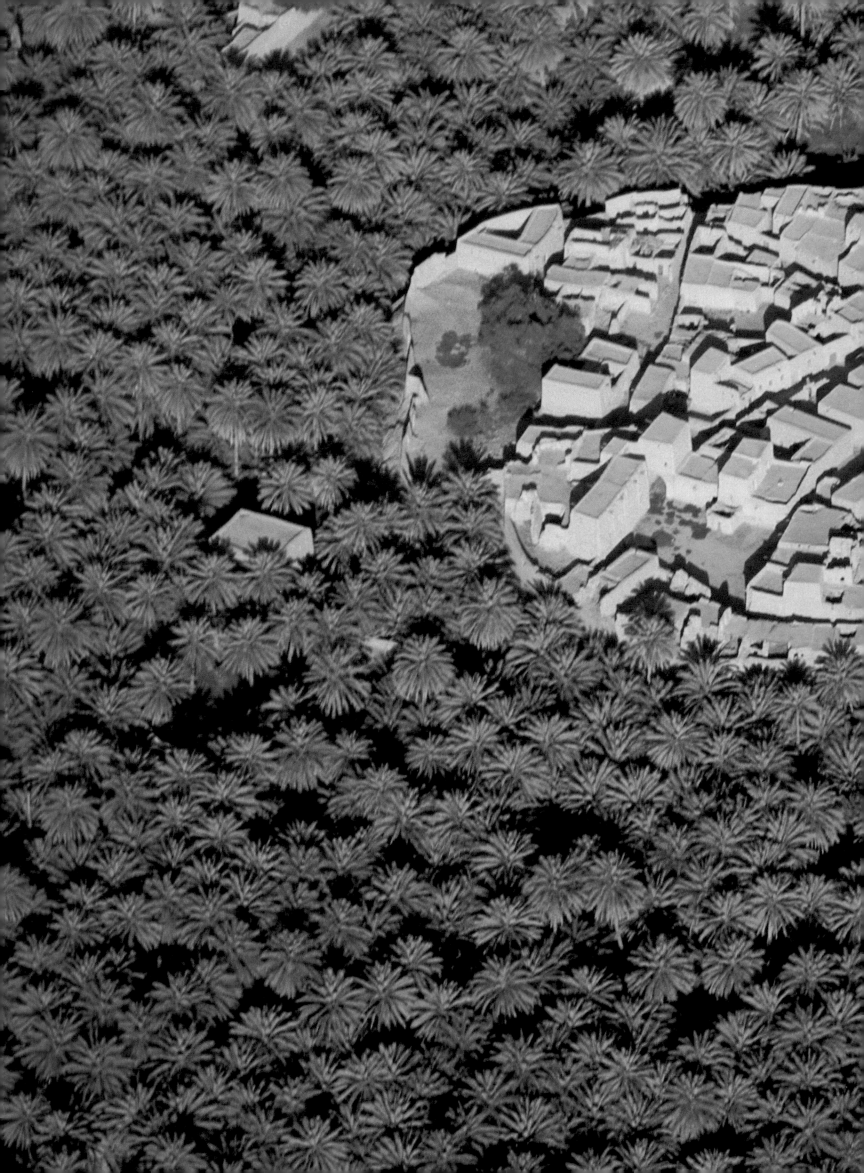

Introduction

5·9·89
09452

Viewed from space, the Sultanate of Oman appears as the edge of a peninsula, at the same time both bridge and barrier to three continents. Lying on the south-eastern edge of the Arabian Peninsula, which was formed when the ancient continent of Gwondonoland split and drifted apart, it is now flanked by the Arabian Sea to the north, the Gulf of Oman and Indian Ocean to the east and the Red Sea to the south.

Millennia ago, this bridge carried ancient forms of elephant, lion and rhinoceros on their migration from Africa to India and Europe. Much later, following in the footsteps of the animals, came man who found that he too had to cross or go round ancient Oman.

When the ancient civilisations of China, India, Egypt and Europe began to trade, the Arabian Peninsula became the crossroads of the ancient world. The need to cross it led to the domestication of the camel over 3,000 years ago. For centuries that followed, camel caravans criss-crossed the peninsula from Dhofar to Ubar and on to Petra and from Sohar to Bahrain.

The need to go around the peninsula led men to the sea, in the process evolving the seamanship, navigation and boat-building for which Oman is renowned. Ras Al Hadd, the most easterly landfall of the peninsula, became the turning point of the seaborne trade, with Sur its pivot.

From high above Oman, the imprint of camel caravans and sailing dhows is not apparent. The whole peninsula is a sepia monochrome colour. Only at a lower altitude does the touch of nature become apparent. From many thousands of feet above Oman, the white and blue surf line encloses majestic 10,000-foot mountains to the north, unexpected greenery to the south, the unique Wahibi Sands and well inland, the vast tracts of stony desert leading to the Empty Quarter, the Rub Al Khali. Lower still, one sees the green flash of alfalfa and date palms, the occasional flash of water and, now and then, the houses of a tiny population in a vast land.

On the coast, more development is visible; the edge of the Battinah Plain, the estuary and dhow yards of Sur and the fertile green centre of the Salalah Plain. In Muscat, the old airstrip at Bait Al Falaj is still visible, now flanked by modern banks.

It was on to this runway that the young Sultan Qaboos landed in 1970 from Salalah to lead his country into the 20th century.

Previous pages: The village of Adam (pages 6 – 7); A wadi near Mazara (pages 8 – 9); Damaniyat Island off Muscat (pages 10 – 11).

For Oman, it was a case of starting almost from scratch — there was little in the way of roads, schools, hospitals, industry or communications. His Majesty first used the new oil wealth to end the Dhofar war and then to put into action his masterly plan that improved the quality of life and the expectations of his people, and put Oman on course to achieve the standing that it enjoys in the world today.

From the earliest days of the country's modern development, His Majesty set a high priority on the protection of the environment. With Oman's potentially rich agricultural and fisheries resources, it was clearly essential to take practical steps against pollution and to protect the countryside which by its stark beauty and romantic fortified villages, offered the prospect of a tourist industry that would make a substantial contribution to the country's income.

Shortly after his accession, Sultan Qaboos appointed his own personal advisor to research problems regarding the environment. In 1974, the first laws concerning environmental affairs were issued, followed closely by further laws defining the territorial waters of the Sultanate.

The establishment of the Council for the Conservation of the Environment and Prevention of Pollution (CCEPP) in 1979 was a significant step toward the achievement of proper environmental control. The chairmanship is held by His Majesty to underline its importance and to provide a strong incentive. In 1984, a Royal Decree established the Ministry of Environment with His Highness Sayyid Shabib bin Taimour Al Said as Minister. The new Ministry was assigned the responsibility for implementing the national plan for the environment and the laws governing the CCEPP. The Ministry also coordinates agencies to deal with emergency cases of pollution.

Oman has valuable coastal and deep water fisheries to protect. Extensive aerial photographic surveys of Omani coastline have been completed to prepare a coastal conservation plan and to control disposal of hazardous wastes. The Ministry is actively involved in increasing public awareness about the environment in collaboration with the Ministry of Education and Sultan Qaboos University which includes environmental sciences in its syllabi. Omani nationals are being trained in several environmental organisations.

13

In the field of nature conservation and the protection of natural resources, a system of nature conservation areas has been prepared for the Sultanate by the International Union for the Conservation of Nature (IUCN). The primary objective of the strategy is to produce an overall development programme to ensure the perpetual availability of renewable water, wildlife and land resources. A new department of National Conservation Strategy (NCS) is being established within the Ministry of the Environment to execute the plan.

Much has already been done to preserve the fauna and flora of Oman. National protected areas both on land and sea have been designated and endangered animals such as the Arabian Tahr and several species of turtle are now thriving in protected places. The re-introduction of the oryx, which had become extinct in Oman in 1972, has been most successfully accomplished. The establishment of the Captive Breeding Centre at Bait Al Birkha by His Majesty recently achieved its most significant milestone when leopards, caught in Jebel Qara, produced offspring for the first time in captivity.

The Sultanate is also rich in history and historic remains covering several thousand years. Oman is one of the few countries in the world to have a Ministry of National Heritage and Culture. The achievements of the Ministry are visible everywhere, from the restoration of Oman's forts and archaeological sites, the establishment of superb museums to the collection and collation of ancient books and manuscripts and the encouragement of traditional handicrafts. Research information is published in *The Journal of Oman Studies*. The Ministry maintains a close contact with Unesco which recently classified both Bahla Fort and the necropolis of Bat near Ibri as World Heritage sites, and the ancient town of Qalhat is being considered.

The successful restoration of historic forts and buildings has been a considerable undertaking. The castle of Jabrin, originally built by Bilarub bin Sultan in the 17th century as a residential palace, is one of the treasures of Omani architecture and has been completely restored. Restoration of the forts of Nizwa, Hazm, Bidbid and Barka has also been completed and the magnificent fort at Rustaq, which guards the approaches to Jebel Akhdar has been carefully restored.

The most visible forts, those of Jalali and Mirani at Muscat and that of Muttrah above the Corniche, have been restored on their superb sites.

Such achievements have only been possible with foresight and direction from the highest level. During the past 15 years, His Majesty Sultan Qaboos has travelled throughout his country as perhaps no other modern ruler has done. Travelling extensively by Royal Flight helicopters, often in conjunction with the annual "Meet the People" tour in the interior and also from the Royal yachts along the coastline of Oman, His Majesty has been able to see first-hand the needs, and celebrate the accomplishments

Ten years ago, the available maps were being outstripped by new developments and the need for more precise information about helicopter landing sites became necessary. Landing site photographs were initially taken by individual units but as His Majesty's flying visits became more frequent and wide-ranging, more units became involved. The Royal Flight, the Royal Air Force of Oman and the Royal Oman Police Air Wing agreed to share information and photographs and a common landing site directory was published. At the same time the National Survey Authority was racing to keep an accurate track of developments for new map production and joined the exchange. Thereafter and to this day, pilots photograph landing sites throughout Oman and distribute the results.

The sheer diversity of visits by His Majesty has resulted in a directory that now fills more than 15 volumes, though now with the easy availability of satellite photographs, the pace is slowing. Photographs from the French "Spot" satellite form the basis of a new geological atlas of Oman, images from Russian satellites help track fishing stocks and fishing boat fleets along the coast, and images from American satellites help geologists in their search for oil-bearing formations in Oman.

It was from photographs originally taken from the Space Shuttle *Challenger* in 1984 that the lost city of Ubar has been tentatively rediscovered. His Majesty originally backed the project in 1984 when he was first shown the pictures taken from space. The view from above Oman once again unlocks the secrets of a lost city to provide the missing link between the trading cities of Sumurhan and Petra.

The natural environment supports life 24 hours a day, year in and year out, in a colourful mosaic of activity; it is as diverse and vibrant as any thriving entity. In this collection of photographs many years are compressed into a single day to represent a cross-section of activity in Oman every day of the year. These images offer a glimpse of the very many facets of Oman, from the traditional to the highly technical, a blend of heritage and environment that is unique in the Arabian Peninsula and the world.

Dawn

6 am

The rising sun breaks the meniscus of the Gulf of Oman. Throughout Oman, the light of a new day illuminates the activities of early risers. A fisherman in a simple craft made of the fronds from a date palm tree woven together, and powered by a modern outboard motor, leaves the shore. Inland, a man gathers ghaf to feed his goats. Offshore, the islands of the Kuria Muria group take shape under a banner of monsoon clouds.

6.15 am

The new dawn has reached Jebel Qara, trailing long shadows from the mosque and school at Tawi Attair. A helicopter crewman looks out over the jebels where morning mist evaporates as the temperature rapidly rises. After the three-month monsoon, the jebel grasses rapidly burn off. To conserve the precious grass, herdsmen have built large store enclosures that exclude animals until later in the season.

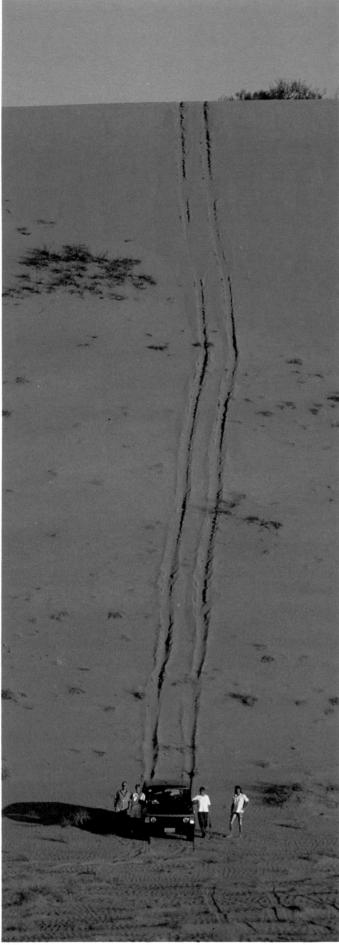

6.30 am

Early morning travellers hurry to beat the soaring, searing desert heat. In the Wahiba Sands, a vast and unique desert environment, between May and September the monsoon winds bring moisture in the form of mists across the land each night. The mists quickly disappear in the heat of the sun but leave sufficient moisture to nurture the vegetation of the sands. In contrast, a deep pool in Wadi Daiqa entices a young tourist into making a dramatic 30-metre plunge.

6.45 am

A trading dhow has left the Dhofar port of Sudh en route to the Kuria Muria Islands to collect the week's catch of fish, frozen in the new government freezer plant. Three hundred kilometres north of Sudh lie the endless sand dunes of the Rub Al Khali — the 'Empty Quarter' — which skirt the western border of Oman. This ocean of sand measures about 1,800 kilometres by 600 kilometres and stretches across southern Saudi Arabia, from the northern mountains of Jebel Akhdar to Yemen. It is one of the world's most extreme deserts, a place where few plants and animals can be found and where no permanent settlements exist. The Rub Al Khali is a closed geological basin with a self-contained drainage system. As a result, the upper soil stratum between the dunes is a brittle mixture of salt and mud called sabka. Travel is extremely difficult yet in this area, satellite photographs have revealed the lost city of Ubar which disappeared in the sands when the need for camel caravans carrying frankincense between Sumurkhan, near present-day Salalah, and Petra lapsed some 1,600 years ago.

7 am

*The sun is now high over the
monsoon clouds of Dhofar. To the
north in Muscat, a Puma helicopter
of The Royal Flight plays a
high-technology part in the
restoration of Oman's heritage.
When work on Fort Jalali was
almost complete, the
carefully-restored canons, 300 years
old and each weighing two tons,
were air-lifted back into the fort,
positioned onto gun carriages and
wheeled back into their original
positions in the gun gallery.*

7.15 am

The training ship Shabab Oman (Youth of Oman) leaves Salalah en route for the United States on a goodwill voyage. The pride of the Sultan of Oman's Navy, the three-masted barquentine has a permanent complement of five officers and 18 ratings and has accommodation for 31 trainees. On the trip to North America five trainee crews had the opportunity to put their seamanship to the test. In this way, Shabab Oman, one of the largest wooden-hulled ships in the world still in active service, plays an important role in helping pass on to future generations the proud Omani seagoing tradition.

7.30 am

At Al Khowd, near Seeb, tiny figures give scale to the vast recharge dam filled by recent rain. The flood waters storm down from Wadi Sumail and while most of the water is retained, sufficient pours out to give early morning travellers a muddy wash. Before the dam was built, the roads around Seeb would be rendered impassable by such a flood. In addition, many millions of cubic metres of water would be lost to the open sea. Today many other such dams are being built along the Battinah Plain in an effort to recharge the aquifers and stop salt water intrusion which, unchecked, was slowly destroying many valuable date palm groves along the coast.

7.45 am

Standing at 2000 metres above sea level, on the route between Wadi Shab and Sumayyan, ancient tombs which have survived for nearly 4,000 years were discovered by chance by the author. The publication of the above photograph in the first edition of this book attracted the attention of international archaeologists, leading to further study of this important find. At sea level, human skeletons thought to be of a similar age to the tombs, have been found in a shallow grave on a headland at Qurm near Muscat. Meanwhile, the timelessness of the Devil's Gap at Wadi Daiqa has the awesome quality of having watched it all.

8 am

At a time when the morning's work for many Omanis is just beginning, that of the fishermen is almost complete. All around the coast of Oman, fishermen return to the shore to supply the fish souks. One fishing boat streaks toward the sand bar to cross into Khor Muscat. Only fishing boats have a sufficiently shallow draught to cross the bar.

8.15 am

Children at a school in Sohar start their day by singing the national anthem. A Puma helicopter of The Royal Flight lowers a modern generating system into an otherwise inaccessible location within the renovated Fort Jalali.
Overleaf, at 8.30 precisely, the Boeing 747 of The Royal Flight flies in salute over the Royal Palace in Muscat. In the Khor, the Royal Dhow rides at anchor.

8.45 am

Water flows along the falaj system through the ruins of the fort at Birkat Al Mawz. The spring-fed falaj is thought to be several hundred years old and has supplied water 24 hours a day since first constructed. The water is rationed along its lower course to feed date plantations where ox ploughs are used to cultivate every possible patch of land. In Jebel Qara, a Jabali tribesman shoulders a .303 Enfield rifle amidst his goat herd. The rifle is not simply for decoration; hyenas and leopards living in the hills prey on unguarded goats.

Morning

9 am

Billowing monsoon clouds pour over Jebel Qara depositing rain which in turn feeds spectacular waterfalls. At Al Ashkharah, villagers examine the morning catch on the beach. A new fishing dhow is under construction beneath a barasti awning while huris and more modern glass fibre fishing boats lie drawn upon the sand.

9.15 am

*Jabali tribesmen have gathered their
many hundreds of camels at the wells
on Nahiz Heights above Salalah.
Here the fierce-looking men take a
morning tea break. A passing tourist
accepts an invitation to try a frothy
bowl of camel's milk....
to the amusement of all.*

9.30 am

The Qurm Nature Reserve forms a wedge between the villas on Qurm Heights and the new ministerial buildings. Inset, the brown waters of a flash flood discolour the sparkling blue of the Gulf of Oman.

9.45 am

Spring-fed terraces of onions, garlic, alfalfa and even roses climb the steep wadis in Jebel Akhdar near the Saiq plateau. The village of Shurayjah is perched on barren rocks above the cultivated terraces. The houses are built on top of each other, making the narrow streets into a system of tunnels into which an occasional shaft of light illuminates an elder hill tribesman.
The sweeping Corniche protects the preserved merchant houses of Muttrah and is itself protected by the renovated fort.

10 am

*The Jebel Akhdar range sweeps
down from the Straights of Hormuz
in northern Oman in a long crescent
to Sur. Here at Wadi Shab, ancient
rainfall has cut a magnificent valley;
the shingle beach at its outflow is
often breached by flash floods.
Travellers and tourists who wish to
explore the wadi must first wade
across the permanent lake or pay the
ferryman. The wadi provides access
for villagers living on the plateau
above Shab. Tourists are rewarded
by a succession of spectacular pools
and waterfalls.*
*Overleaf, a modern display of Omani
seamanship as captains of
high-speed craft race toward
Muscat.*

10.30 am

High above Tanuf, where a modern plant bottles the mountain spring water, live hardy mountain people on the sides of vertical drops of several hundred metres. The modest inhabitants stayed indoors when the helicopter flew past, their presence betrayed by polished kitchen utensils hanging ready for use. On the plain below, a magnificent example of a restored fort can be seen at Falaij, just one of the many buildings being preserved throughout Oman.

10.45 am

*A camel train turns back time as it moves along a
traditional track up Wadi Afal in Dhofar, forcing a
temporary halt to modern road construction. The
Jabali tribesman has a good reason to smile, for when
the new road is finished, his access to the markets in
Salalah will be much easier and it is likely that he will
transport his camels in the back of a pickup truck.*

11 am

Whales are a common sight along the coast of Oman.
Recent research has revealed that whales navigate
using lines of magnetic variation which in the vicinity
of Oman lie parallel to the coast from Salalah to Ras
Al Hadd. This explains why many whales are observed
in that area, yet few are seen around the headland
toward Muscat. Unlike whales, sea captains have no
intuition to help with navigation and all along the
coast of Oman lie wrecks which attest to the failure of
man-made instrumentation.

11.15 am

People give scale to the 10,000-foot mountains of Oman. The helicopter hovers near a natural arch on the steep ridgeline of Jebel Al Umr in Dhofar. Far below lies Saleh's Mosque and Tomb in a location so inaccessible that a helicopter pad has been built to provide regular access. In Wadi Tiwi, donkey riders leave the tranquil pools and palm plantations for a six-hour trek to their village at the head of the wadi. Overleaf, a traditional hand cast net soars over the surf while (inset) the hand-thrown nets of shrimp fishermen compete with swooping seabirds near the island of Mahawt.

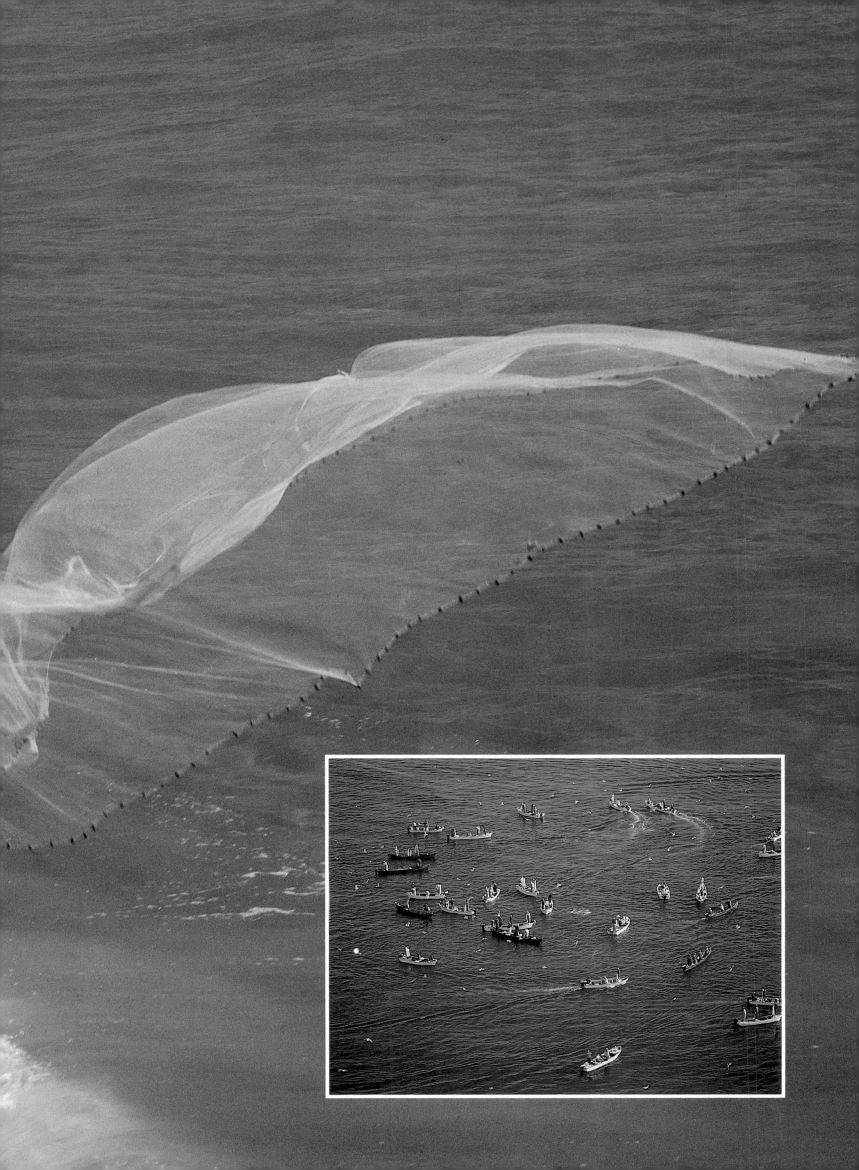

11.45 am

A helicopter flies over the village and disused airfield at Ras Al Hadd, the most easterly point of the Arabian Peninsula and the turning point for a majestic trading dhow under sail. Turning a sailing dhow onto a new course is a complicated manoeuvre known as "wearing ship". Once the procedure is complete, the dhow captain can relax once more with his pipe.

12.15 pm

Nizwah's imposing citadel, a masterpiece of fortification, dominates this old capital of Oman as much from the air as it does from the ground. It was built by Imam Sultan Ibn Saif, who finally ejected the Portuguese from Muscat in 1650, and stands 30 metres high and some 36 metres across. Around it, the modern town of Nizwah, crossroads of the interior, goes about its business, while inside the fortress, the curator-guard poses on the parapet, proudly wearing his khunjar. This curved dagger with it decorated sheath is a traditional part of an Omani man's apparel, though the additional uses to which it is sometimes put are strictly modern.

67

12.30 pm

The call to mid-day Adhar prayers is heard across Oman. The mosque at Misfah is perched on a massive rock to permit date palm cultivation all around. Inside the shadowy maze of Misfah, a lady carries water from the falaj.
Overleaf, thousands of migrating cormorants cover the sea near Masirah. Further south the cormorants converge on the barren waterless island of Hamar An Nafur, off the coast near Duqm, while a masked booby prepares to dive for fish near the Kuria Muria Islands.

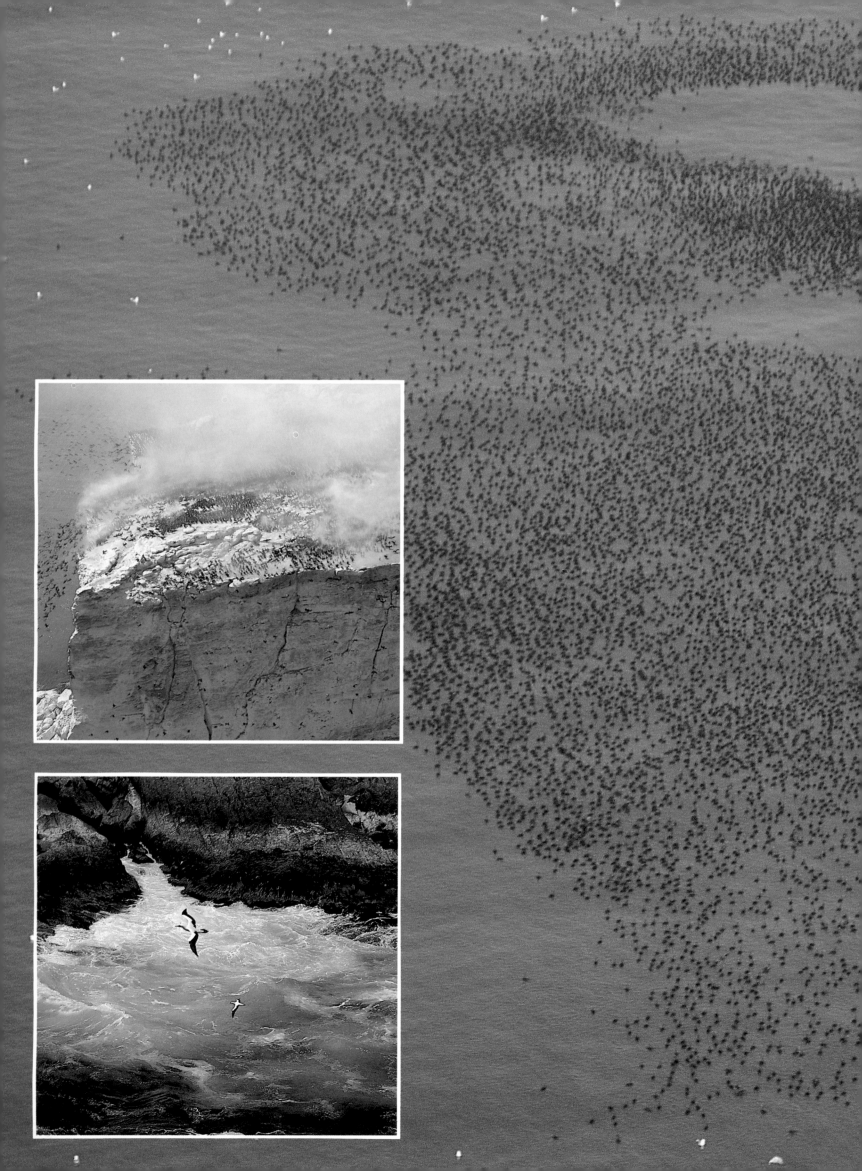

1.15 pm

The deserted ruins of Qalhat silently bake in the early afternoon heat. The ancestral home of the Persian King of Hormuz, Qalhat had replaced Sohar in importance in the 14th and 15th centuries. It was destroyed by the Portuguese in 1508 and today only the Bibi Maryam Tomb remains standing. Qalhat is being considered by Unesco for inclusion on the World Heritage List.

1.30 pm

High on Jebel Akhdar live shepherds known as Shawawi who keep goats, sheep and donkeys. The villagers use a ground loom to weave rugs in patterns of either brown and white, from natural wool, or red and black. The red colour is achieved by dying with madder, a rich colouring brought by dhow from India, and forms a startling backdrop to the traditional weapons found in the jebel.

77

1.45 pm

Tourists stand on a cliff overlooking the pools of Ayun, a series of large and deep lakes located some 30 kilometres north of Salalah. Groups can now ride in four-wheel-drive vehicles across the barren countryside called the Nedj where only camels and frankincense trees exist. A short walk leads down to the cliffs above the water and a natural serenity disturbed only by the calls of birds. A thousand kilometres to the north, a dhow lies within the sheltered arms of Bander Jissa.

2 pm

A dhow floats motionless on the crystal-clear waters off Bar Al Hikman. Oman's coastline, so rich in fish and plant life, is the subject of an extensive survey conducted for the Coastal Zone Management Plan. The shallow water at Bar Al Hikman conceals many square kilometres of untouched coral, teeming with fishlife and turtles. A local fisherman took Dr Rodney Salm, project coordinator, out over the coral to enable him to make a closer underwater inspection. The local fishermen, the Hikmanis, treat the shallow waters above the coral as their larder in case bad weather prevents them from fishing in deeper water. Overleaf, a diesel-powered trading dhow filled to the brim with sheep, pounds through a rough monsoon sea. In the sheltered channel between Masirah and the mainland, another trading dhow acts as a floating fresh meat market for local fishermen from Masirah.

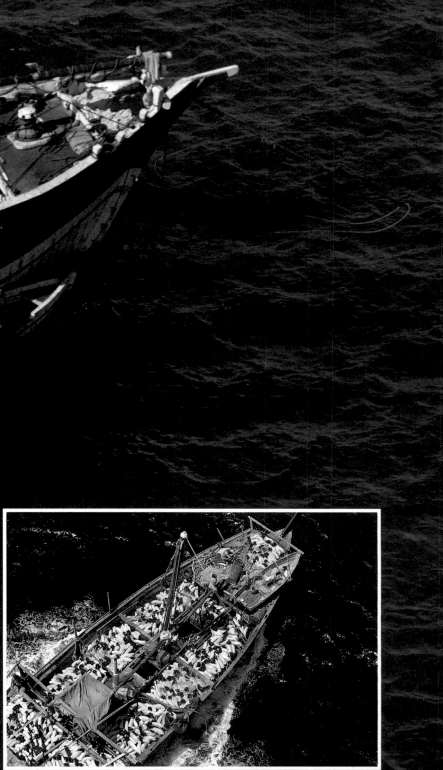

2.30 pm

Modern graded roads provide access to villages such as Das Sawda on Jebel Akhdar where tourists are now able to drive and buy rugs from the mountain weavers. It is customary to give lifts to any traveller on the mountains. In southern Oman, a road cutting from the plateau down to the bay at Shuwaymiyah has reduced an arduous journey of several days to a few hours.

2.45 pm

*A rock carving in Wadi Tanuf,
depicting extinct animals, is one of
the many ancient carvings throughout
Oman that prove it once served as a
land bridge between continents.
On the gravel plain of the Jiddat Al
Harrisis, the almost extinct oryx has
been reintroduced with great
success, following a world-wide
effort to re-establish the animal in
its native domain.
The Omani heritage is also being
preserved by young ladies who still
wear traditional dress, and by the
restoration work being done on old
forts, as at Rustaq where the lady is
standing next to a magnificent
renovated door.*

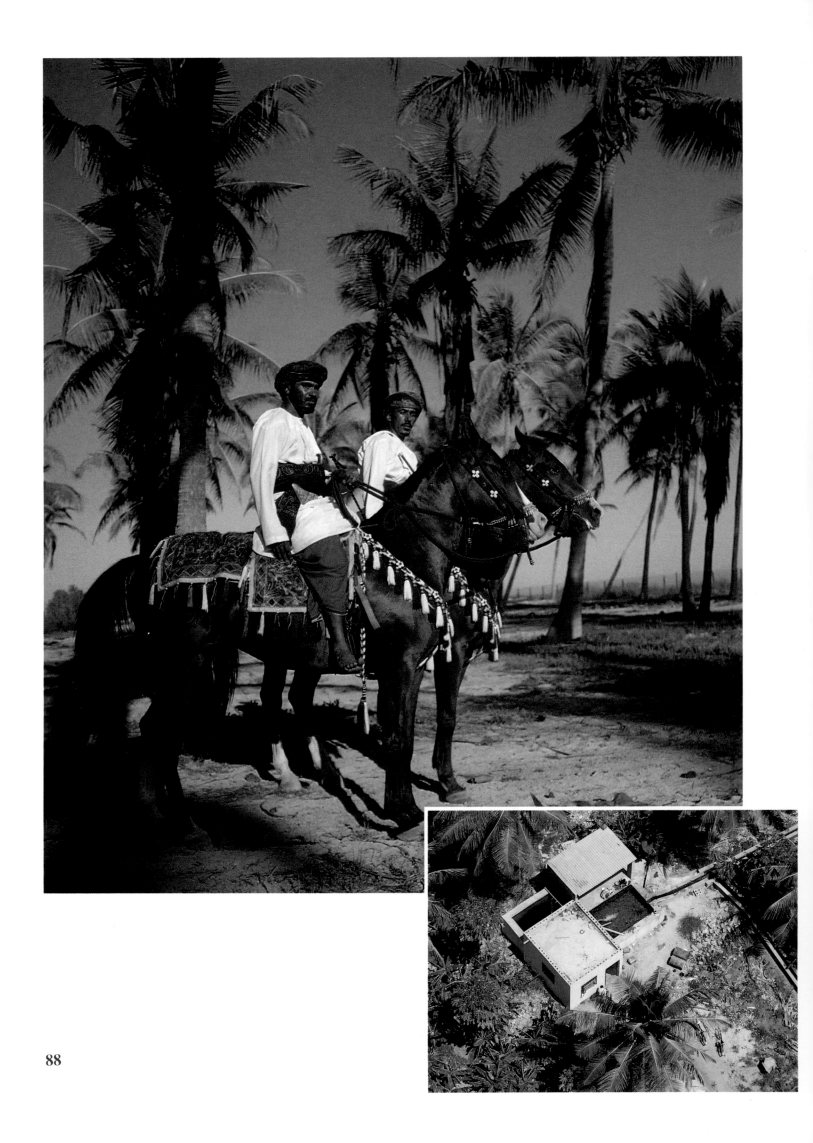

3 pm

The remarkable greenery in Salalah is the result of the summer south-west monsoon. Deep offshore currents force an upwelling of cold water in the Indian Ocean. When warm moist air is pushed inland over the cool sea surface, condensation takes place, forming extensive stratus cloud formation and precipitation on Jebel Qara. The friendly people of Salalah have a respite from the harsh summer sun under the monsoon clouds and are now joined by many visitors from the United Arab Emirates and Saudi Arabia who flock to Salalah for the cool summer season.
Overleaf, donkeys carry a Bedu woman in the Wahiba sands and an old man in the mountains.

3.30 pm

In the mid-afternoon heat, when the people of Oman have sought shelter and rest, the coastline of Oman lies untouched, unspoiled and spectacular. Long white beaches stretch for hundreds of kilometres, flanked by a sparkling blue sea and coral reefs. In the south, dramatic cliffs fall into the sea. Near Ghubbat Hashish, an underwater area of seagrass provides food for turtles and prawns, while further north the Wahiba Sands meet the sea. As a result of the exhaustive work carried out under the Coastal Zone Management Plan, the value of the coastline is being appreciated as a vital part of Oman's environmental heritage.

3.45 pm

*Drums of aviation fuel are
positioned throughout Oman to
facilitate the operation of both fixed
wing aircraft and helicopters of The
Royal Air Force of Oman, The Royal
Oman Police Air Wing and The
Royal Flight. Aircraft arriving and
refuelling at remote spots such as
Duqm signify to the Bedu a special
medical flight or a visit by a
minister. Masked women wait
patiently for the empty fuel drums
which, when cleaned, are used for
storing water. Capt Nick Mylne,
well-known Arabist and fuel
planning expert of The Royal Flight,
talks to.a Duqm elder.*

Afternoon

4 pm

*Water found by accident by the Petroleum
Development Organisation near Marmul is put to
dramatic use on an experimental farm. In the Wahiba
Sands are several wells sufficient only for a sparse
population of Bedu and their goats.*

4.15 pm

In previous centuries, Oman was renowned for the excellence of its horses. Many were exported, mainly to India, where they were used as mounts for the cavalry regiments. The breed reached its zenith during the reign of Said bin Sultan in the 19th century; the beauty of the grey mare and black stallion he presented to William IV and to Queen Victoria on the occasion of their coronations is legendary. Horse-breeding in Oman decreased in the early 20th century due to severe drought. After his accession in 1970, HM Sultan Qaboos made great efforts to re-establish Oman as a breeder of fine Arabian horses, by opening the Royal Stud in Salalah and importing stallions and mares. Today Arab horses are once more a part of every day life. Competitive events are staged during the winter season at Seeb and endurance events are staged in many walyats. Along the beach in Salalah, the Arab stud horses Robatiyah and Sari Alehl are being exercised in traditional harness.

5 pm

*Three young ladies in their traditional finery happily
pose for a family portrait by a bubbling falaj near
Seeb. At Muscat, the late afternoon sun catches the
face of a fisherman pulling in his net.*

5.15 pm

At Sur, dhow-building continues to thrive. Across the creek lies Al Bat'h Bay where little has changed for hundreds of years. On the Al Aija shore sits Bait Sarrai, home of Abdullah Khamis Al Sarrai who was a dhow captain until 1978. Today his son is an aircraft engineer working on modern Boeing jets but he still returns with his wife and son to visit the family home to enjoy a traditional weekend with his father. On the shore below the house, Sabeet bin Khamis bin Faraj Al Alawi continues to build dhows using traditional methods; his work is famous throughout the Gulf.

107

5.30 pm

The genteel sounds of the harp blend with the tinkle of cups as afternoon tea is served in the atrium of the Al Bustan Palace Hotel. Outside, the blue sea, white beach, green coconut palms, gold-topped dome against the dark rocks and the flash of red tennis courts underline the magnificent setting. This classic combination of Islamic architecture in a dramatic environment has culminated in the hotel's being voted the Best Hotel in the World by Leaders magazine. Out in the bay, against the backdrop of the hotel, a fisherman casts his net in the traditional way and fills baskets made from palm fronds with a catch of sardines.

109

5.45 pm

Dark rocky hills surround Muttrah and Mina Qaboos harbour where tugs and cargo ships bask in the early evening sunlight. In the souk, dark figures pass a silversmith's shop where a cat wearing a silver necklace keeps watch on traditional silver coffee pots and a bowl of frankincense.

Evening

6 pm

Far to the west, the ruins of Bahla Fort stand out in the cross-lighting. The fort, classified by Unesco as an endangered monument, has had international funds allocated toward its restoration. It dates from pre-Islamic times, though the present fort was probably built by the Persians. The town of Bahla is surrounded by a fortified wall similar in construction to that of Sumerian cities. Beyond the deserted fort, the roof of the souk conceals a myriad shops and the flames of a khunjar maker. Further back in the date plantation, potters' kilns cool in the deep shadows before the baked pots can be removed.

6.15 pm

As the sun descends, the fish rise and while one fisherman casts a lobster pot, another carries home his catch on a paddle. In Fanjah, a sword dancer leaps into the air while a date harvester climbs at a more gentle pace to his crop. In Salalah, four boys enjoy the milk from fresh coconuts on the beach.

6.30 pm

The creeping shadow of dusk gradually envelopes the business district that has been built during the last 20 years. In 1970, only a runway and the fort at Bait Al Falaj were visible in the Ruwi valley. Today banks line each side of the old runway and the roar of traffic fills the broad wadi.

6.45 pm

In Buraimi, a vast oasis that borders the United Arab Emirates, restoration of the fort is almost complete. In Wadi Jizzi, footballers with long shadows take advantage of cooler evening temperatures, as do shoppers in the souk as Sumail.

7 pm

A group of junior fishermen in a houri dugout canoe are oblivious to the spectacle of the sun touching the sea west of Masirah. In the darkness that follows, a 20th century display of laser light bursts from a 16th century fort in Muscat.
Overleaf, the Ruwi valley glows with interwoven necklaces of light as Omanis return home at the end of the day.

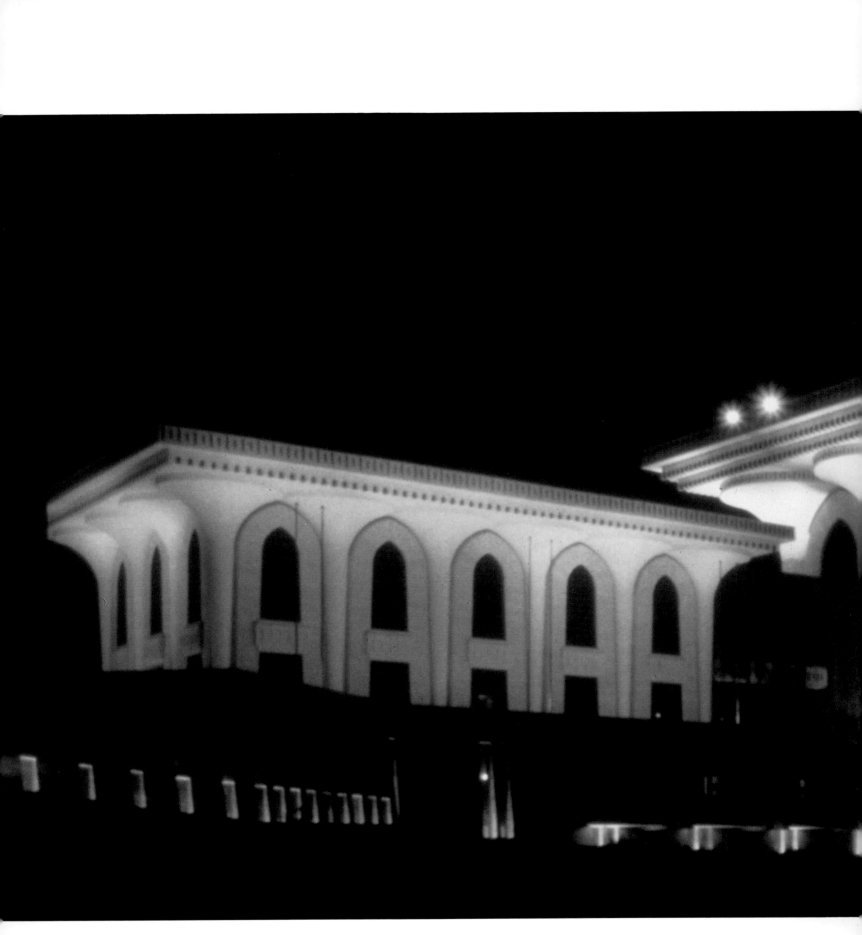

8 pm

The lights from the palace of His Majesty Sultan Qaboos shine out over a tranquil sea, reflecting 20 years of progress and achievement in a land blessed with a rich heritage and an appreciation of its value now and to future generations.

Acknowledgements

Taking an aerial photograph is relatively simple since focus is set at infinity and the highest possible shutter speed is used to eliminate vibration. The true skill is that of the pilot who can fly one into the right position. I am grateful for having had the pleasure of flying with Bill Burborough, Chris Brotherton, Phil Bleasdale, Tony Horsey, Baz Longhurst, Nick Mylne, Jimmy Millar, Peter Norton, Phil Stevens, Philip Todd and Chris Warne of The Royal Flight; David Sutcliffe, Richard Shuttleworth and Randy Mains of The Royal Oman Police Air Wing; John Smith and the late David Payne of The Royal Air Force of Oman; and Richard Owen of Gulf Helicopters.

My special thanks to Duncan Donaldson and Kevin Smith of The Royal Flight who have been flying me into classic photographic positions for almost 20 years and whose joint flying skills resulted in the photo on page 50-51 which was taken with a wide-angle lens.

My thanks also to my fellow crew members, Saud, Saif, Mansour, Said, Saad, Humaid, Dougal Lawton and the late Mohammed Moosa for their comradeship in the air. My gratitude also goes to all the many Omani ladies, gentlemen and children whose hospitality and patient replies to my endless questions about Oman made our 10-year tour a most happy period.

To my fellow photographers Mel Conway, John Davies, Said Al Harthy, Alan Hillyer, Mike Jones, Moh'd Kharusi, Lou Lyddon, Moh'd Mustapha, Larry Major, Marc Mallett, Ted Marriott, Bob Spiteri and Sam Sloan go thanks for their companionship and contributions.

Many thanks to Ralph and Elizabeth Daly who provided the spark that developed into this book, to Andrew and Sheila Graham of BP Middle East who made it possible and to Chuck Grieve of Motivate Publishing for his guidance.

My heartfelt thanks to my children Marc, Kerri, Robert, Simone, Nicholas and William and my wife Christine who endured sandstorms, floods, drives and climbs to places where no expatriate had been before. With only one refusal "to go any further" in eight years, I can hardly complain.

And finally, thanks to BP Middle East, whose support and encouragement made publication of this book possible.

The author

Yorkshire-born John Nowell traces his interest in the environment to his youth. A member of the Explorers Club at Morley Grammar school, he also spent school holidays exploring the Grampian Mountains in Scotland, the English Lake District and the mountains of Snowdonia in Wales.

After school, John joined the Royal Air Force and began a 30-year flying career; in all he has flown more than 10,000 hours in helicopters, jets, anti-submarine bombers, seaplanes and the much more environmentally genteel gliders and balloons. During his 10-year stay in Oman his passengers included many visiting heads of state.

John met his wife Christine in Singapore, and it was she who introduced him to photography. His work has been published around the world, and displayed in Royal households and Ministries in Oman. He was made a Licentiate of the Royal Photographic Society in August, 1990, on the basis of pictures from this book.

He and his wife and their six children now live in Windemere, near Orlando, Florida.

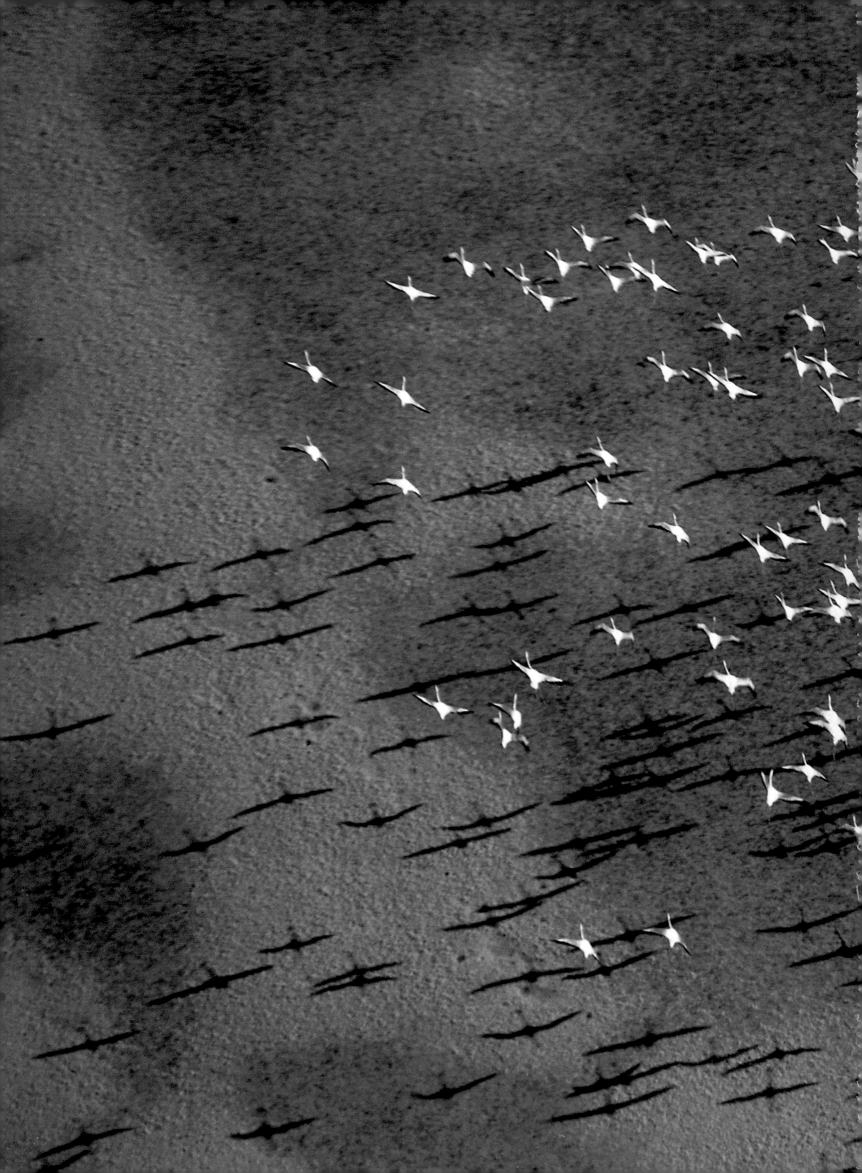